ABOUT THE AUTHOR

Ruth Stenerson writes this book out of many years' experience as a teacher and author. After teaching high school for seven years, she attained a master's degree in English from the University of North Dakota, Grand Forks. She presently serves as associate professor of English at Bemidji State University (BSU) in Bemidji, Minnesota. Her articles have appeared in various Christian journals and she has written devotional books. Her work has also been published in the *Minnesota English Journal*. She wrote and compiled a *Handbook for the Bible as Literature* which is used as the text for a course she teaches at BSU.

Bible Readings for Students is Stenerson's third volume in this devotional series. She is also the author of *Bible Readings for Teachers* and *Bible Readings for Singles*.

Bible Readings
FOR STUDENTS

Bible Readings

FOR STUDENTS

Ruth Stenerson

AUGSBURG Publishing House • Minneapolis

BIBLE READINGS FOR STUDENTS

Copyright © 1986 Augsburg Publishing House

Scripture quotations unless otherwise noted are from the Holy Bible: New International Version. Copyright 1978 by the New York International Bible Society. Used by permission of Zondervan Bible Publishers.

Scripture quotations marked TEV are from the Good News Bible, Today's English Version, copyright 1966, 1971, 1976 by American Bible Society. Used by permission.

Library of Congress Cataloging-in-Publication Data

Stenerson, Ruth.
    BIBLE READINGS FOR STUDENTS.

    1. College students—Prayer-books and devotions—
English. I. Title.
BV4850.S74 1986   242'.634   85-30771
ISBN 0-8066-2190-7

Manufactured in the U.S.A.   APH 10-0691

1 2 3 4 5 6 7 8 9 0 1 2 3 4 5 6 7 8 9

To the faculty,
students, and staff
with whom I have had fellowship
through my years of college teaching
—and especially to Phil and Betty Sauer,
whose friendship has been a constant
stimulation and support.

PREFACE

"Don't let anyone look down on you because you are young but set an example for the believers in speech, in life, in love, in faith, and in purity" (1 Tim. 4:12).

To be an example in word, action, and attitude is not easy. It can be especially difficult in the intellectual world, whether one is at a church college or a secular university.

Some expect a college or university campus to be a center for doubt and spiritual darkness, a place where people lose their faith or find it watered down. This need not happen if one's faith is nourished by a regular devotional life and by Christian fellowship. When prayer is left behind, spiritual life will atrophy. When the Bible is seldom read, the word of love and assurance grows hard to hear. When Christian fellowship is ignored, we walk single file on a road on which God meant us to travel together.

When using this book, please be sure to read the Bible selections. Without them the meditations will be less meaningful. I hope that these pages will be a means of bringing you who are living your college years to the Bible day by day, of stimulating thought about what it means to be a Christian student in the intellectual world, of reminding you that a life that is not deepening and growing is in danger of regressing, of making habitual a life of faith well exercised in the Word and prayer. To that end, God bless you!

■ ALL TRUTH IS HIS

John 1:1-18: "Grace and truth came through Jesus Christ" (v. 17).

One of the most vital principles for the Christian who lives in the society of intellectuals is that all truth belongs to God. If all truth belongs to God, and I belong to God, then I have nothing to fear from the truth. When intellectual problems and doubts arise, they are the result of our incomplete picture of truth. Human ideas about what is truth do change.

Much that is asserted to be true in the intellectual world is simply the best possible theory at the time. Some theories when new are exciting and seem to sweep all before them, often being pushed beyond their limits.

In many areas of learning we can afford to wait for further illumination. Theories come and go, even when all the evidence has seemed to be in. When the picture is complete, no matter how long that may take, we will know for sure that truth comes from God.

 Lord, strengthen my faith and my patience. Help me to remember that faith can hold on even when much of the evidence is still out.

Visit with a Christian professor about what enables a believer to maintain faith in the face of intellectual doubt.

■ REAL COMFORT

Gen. 8:1-12: "God remembered Noah" (v. 1).

I like the Jerusalem Bible rendition of verse 1: "But God had Noah in mind." That connects with my college experience and my constant awareness during those years that my parents "had me in mind." Most college students are aware that while they go to the cafeteria or to their examinations or to the hockey game, there are those at home who "have them in mind."

Those who love us as we go about our student lives often have a way of acting on our behalf. A letter appears in our mailbox, or an unexpected check, or there is the prayer we may know nothing about, the visit, the telephone call that lets us know we are being thought of. And it is good just to know that, as they go about their work, they have us in mind.

How encouraging to know that the God who had Noah in mind after those traumatic weeks has us in mind too—in mind when we are lonely, in mind when there is a big paper due or we are on a panel discussion, or when a big test is scheduled.

 Thank you, Lord, that every day of my life you have me in mind.

Let your family know by some thoughtful word or act that you have them in mind.

■ THE CHAINS OF CONFORMITY

Rom. 12:1-8: "Do not conform any longer to the pattern of this world, but be transformed by the renewing of your mind" (v. 2).

The pressure to conform is felt by all ages of society, but most strongly by the young. High school is probably peak period for such pressures, and girls seem to feel more pressured to conform than boys. Behind it is that very natural, understandable desire to be accepted, liked, and admired. College students have often begun to break the chains of conformity, but the pressures are still there. As evidence, look at those who dislike the taste of beer but gulp it down because that is a conforming way of expressing freedom from home control and similarity to new friends. Some do second-rate work in their studies because their set favors the "gentleman's C."

Conformists often get the desired acceptance and praise that they desire, but they may miss out on some other, more lasting rewards. Conformity is a shackling influence unless it is conformity to God's Spirit at work in our hearts and lives.

 Free me, Lord, from slavery to useless conformity. May I instead conform to your will in my decisions.

Listen in your social contacts today for evidence of people feeling pressures to conform to the group.

■ THE FIRST TRIP HOME

1 Thess. 5:11: ". . . encourage one another and build each other up" (v. 11).

Because going to college is usually tied to coming of age, it often is a time of stress between parents and a son or daughter. No one wants it to be that way; it just is. Perhaps some of the stress is present, hidden under the smiles, when the car is loaded, then unloaded into a dorm room. The student is off into new experiences, exciting and even a bit frightening. Parents try to adjust to an emptier, quieter house. Soon they are expectantly opening their door to their son or daughter home for the first visit or vacation.

What happens when Lori or Larry comes home? Very naturally Lori is eager to hear how her friends going to other colleges are doing. What about Mary, who took a job instead? What's with the good friend who is still a senior in high school? Lori goes off—and off—and off, to find out. Sunday evening she returns to campus, and her parents may not have had a chance for a real visit with her. Neither she nor they are happy about that. Next time will be different.

 Lord, help me nurture my relationship with my family when we are not able to see each other as often as before.

In your plans for your next visit home, set aside a special time just to be with your family.

14

■ THE QUIET HEART

Mark 6:30-32:   "Come with me by yourselves to a
quiet place and get some rest" (v. 31).

Quiet can be a scarce commodity today. Loud
mufflers throb, and motorcycles roar by with radios
blaring. Stereos in dormitory windows entertain
frisbee players. At a construction site jackhammers
pound, and from the freeway sirens scream.

The noise on the shores of Lake Galilee in Jesus'
day would seem like whispers in comparison to our
modern, escalated sounds. But even there, the coming
and the going was so constant that Jesus knew what it
was doing to the ability of his disciples to handle what
was happening around them. His prescription was
solitude—time with him in a quiet place with the
frantic rush shut out. As is often true in our settings,
the quiet didn't last long. The crowds came there too.

All of us need times of quiet to maintain our ability
to function. Jesus summons us from life's frenetic rush
with an invitation to come apart and find our worth in
him, absorbing his serenity and quiet, and refreshing
our spirits with his presence and peace.

 Lord, give me the capacity to rest in the quiet
you can provide in my inner being.

**Seek out a place on campus or near where you live
that can be a retreat for you into the silence your
spirit needs.**

■ GRATEFUL FOR THE GOOD THINGS

Deut. 26:1-11: "You shall rejoice in all the good things the Lord your God has given to you and your household" (v. 11).

Moses and God saw a special need among the people who had been led out from the past, through the desert, and on to their future. They needed to look at their history and remind themselves what God had done. This need was so important that they ritualized it, weaving their response to it into their religious rituals. They recognized that God's dealings with humanity did not begin with them but with their ancestors. Their future would be shaped by God's relationship with those ancestors as well as by the events of their own lives.

We are only partially tied to our past: God has the power to set us free from it to a great degree. But there is much in that past that can enrich us, that can teach us how God led his people then and is willing to lead us today and tomorrow. God is no less interested in us than in the people of Old Testament times.

 Help me, Father, to profit from the past even when I am tempted to think the only important thing is to break free from it.

Do some research into your family history. Can you find instances in which God's leading seemed evident in your family?

■ BEYOND JUDGMENT

Matt. 7:1-5: "For in the same way you judge others, you will be judged" (v. 2).

We are Americans, but also Texans or Californians or Iowans, or 47 other varieties at the same time. We are Christians, but we are also Baptists or Methodists or Lutherans, or members of one of many other denominations. When all of us live together on the same campus, there are many encounters between people of various denominations. In my Bible Literature class, some suspect my Christianity because my denominational affiliation is different from theirs. I know colleagues who have been committed Christians their entire careers who have had students make serious efforts to convert them to another denomination.

Most of us seem to grow up knowing very little about other denominations, their histories, and differences in doctrine from ours. It is therefore easy to be judgmental.

We human beings like to set up walls that make us feel comfortable and keep others excluded. We all come to God by grace. God's grace meets us where we are in our particular needs and makes us all wonderfully welcome.

 Lord, help me to leave judgment in your hands.

Find an opportunity to come to a better understanding of another branch of Christianity by visiting a service or dialoging with someone from that background.

■ NO PROMISE OF A ROSE GARDEN

1 Peter 4:12-19:   "If you suffer as a Christian . . .
praise God that you bear that name" (v. 16).

A campus is not the easiest place to be a committed
Christian. At a Christian college, there is a temptation
to suppose that just being in that environment is
enough. If we are attending a public university, we
know there is constant temptation to set our faith aside
and live as others do, to accept unthinkingly ideas that
do not square with Christian beliefs. At either kind of
school, there is the human temptation to coast, to put
our commitment aside while we conform to the society
around us.

Some people claim that if we are Christians, all our
problems disappear and life becomes one endless
victory party. Jesus, his disciples, and Paul knew
nothing about a trouble-free way of life. They knew
persecution, discouragement, and martyrdom. But
what they also knew, and what we can know too, is
the constant presence and love of God in our daily
experience, whether we are in a difficult setting or an
easy one.

 Lord, may my life on this campus be a time of
constant growth in commitment to you and
resting in your love.

**Find a way to be supportive of someone else on
campus who is going through a difficult experience.**

■ THE FIRST LINE OF DEFENSE

1 Tim. 6:20-21: ". . . guard what has been entrusted to your care" (v. 20).

Professors in both public and private schools are often blamed for the loss of faith among their students. Many young people have come out of freshman classes in philosophy or science with doubts about God and the church.

Certainly, some professors do take pleasure in challenging students' faith. A few may even consider it a victory if a student stops believing in God. But there are many dedicated Christian professors who know that students must think through their views of God and the world very carefully if they are to develop maturity in their faith.

The survival and growth of one's faith actually depends much more on using the spiritual resources of the Bible, prayer, church attendance, and the support of other Christians. It is through these that the Holy Spirit keeps faith alive and well in college. Where prayer and Bible reading are part of each day, we can grow into the firm, well-rooted faith we all desire to have.

 Lord, keep me faithful in my use of your Word and prayer.

Schedule at least 15 minutes into your daily program for Bible reading and prayer.

■ GOD KNOWS YOUR NEEDS

Phil. 4:19:   "God will meet all your needs . . ."
(v. 19).

For many college students, money—or the lack of it—is one of the most daily of problems. The savings you intended to last through the quarter are gone two weeks before finals. A book would be helpful in a course, but you can't spare the money to buy it. The lab fee you hadn't anticipated swallowed the money you needed to pay expenses for a date.

God is concerned about your physical needs. That sounds like a rash statement: there are many who experience basic needs that are not met, and it seems God shows no concern. Do we really have a right to make material requests?

I really believe God has resources to meet our *needs*, though perhaps God will not satisfy all of our *wants*. When finances threaten to defeat you, don't give up. Have a visit with your campus minister. He may know of a low-interest (or even no-interest) loan fund. Talk to a counselor, a financial aid officer, or a favorite professor about your need. You may be surprised how many hands God has on campus.

 Lord, thank you for being concerned about every aspect of my life.

If money isn't one of your problems, give your campus minister $10 to be used for some student who is experiencing financial need.

■ THE SPIRIT OF ADVENTURE

Luke 18:18-30: "No one who has left home . . . for the sake of the kingdom of God will fail to receive many times as much in this age and, in the age to come, eternal life" (vv. 29-30).

Kris was thrilled to tell me she had accepted an invitation to teach English for two years in Papua, New Guinea. Ray said yes eagerly to a contract for teaching migrant children in a school near the Mexican border. Dot applied for the Peace Corps and was accepted for service in Peru.

The job shortage is a concern for college students. Some, for valid reasons, are not vocationally mobile. A nontraditional student, for instance, may need to accept employment near that of a spouse or a supportive family. But many of us can be adventurous and accept the challenge of a job at a distance to fulfill our vocations and serve God and others.

A real satisfaction can be ours by rising to the challenge of the unusual, the demand for the spurt of adventurousness to do the task from which others draw back.

 Lord of my life, give me a healthy dose of daring.

Find a listing of jobs by an organization that works for overseas development and see which of them might fit your interests and field of preparation.

■ OUR NEED FOR FELLOWSHIP

Acts 2:40-47:   "They devoted themselves to the apostles' teaching and to the fellowship, to the breaking of bread and to prayers" (v. 42).

Leaders of sensitivity sessions often use the technique of asking an individual to "fall" limply into the arms of those who encircle him or her. The strong arms of others offer the needed support. So in our spiritual lives: the love and concern and companionship of those who share our faith strengthen and support us.

As Christians we are not meant to be an exclusive subgroup of society who hold ourselves apart from others. We are to be salt and light. But we need association with each other. Many of my happiest associations in college were with those who liked to spend an hour singing together, an afternoon presenting a service at a nursing home, an evening going to a neighboring town to lead a youth program. Some of my most treasured friendships from college teaching are those with Christian students and faculty. We have need for each other, and we find spiritual strength and reinforcement in each other.

 Thank you, Lord, for my Christian friends. May others see in us the meaning of what it is to be part of your family.

Offer your friendship to another Christian student.

■ LIVING WITH CONSEQUENCES

Gen. 3:17-24: "So the Lord God banished him from the Garden of Eden to work the ground from which he had been taken" (v. 23).

Actions have consequences. Adam and Eve learned that lesson with much pain. Their act of disobedience closed the gates of the Garden. We too may find that our actions have closed doors that otherwise would have been open.

An important part of education is learning to reckon with consequences before, not after, the act that brings them upon us. The girl who does not let herself be impregnated does not have to consider abortion. The student who refuses to drink and drive does not have to deal with possible arrest, injury, or death.

There is something very human about supposing that in our case the consequences will get sidetracked, but a delicate vase is still shattered after its owner tells us, "I know you didn't mean to break it." Even God's forgiveness does not always remove consequences, though it can help us to live with them.

 Lord, help me to look carefully at my actions that I may exercise choice about which consequences I want to experience.

Spend a few minutes thinking about the possible consequences of your day-to-day behavior patterns. Are there some negative consequences you could avoid by changing a habit?

■ PROBLEMS AT HOME

Luke 7:1-10: "Say the word, and my servant will be healed" (v. 7).

Many students go through some hectic nights and days worrying about problems at home. These can be painful—marital conflicts between parents, the illness of a family member, financial pressures, disagreements between brothers and sisters. Any of these can make it hard to concentrate on writing a paper or preparing for an exam.

The Roman officer of our text knew there was trouble at home too. A valued servant was ill. The officer drew a glowing compliment from Jesus for his confidence that his servant could be healed even when Jesus was not physically present. "I have not found such great faith," Jesus marveled.

We, too, can believe that the Christ who is with us in our dorm rooms or apartments is also back home with our families, with grandparents in nursing homes, with friends on other campuses, with brothers or sisters in military service. Like the officer, we may with confident faith ask Christ for help.

 Lord, be with those I love at home today.

When friends talk about problems at home, give them a sympathetic ear.

■ USING YOUR TALENTS

Matt. 25:14-30: "It will be like a man going on a journey, who called his servants and entrusted his property to them . . . each according to his ability" (vv. 14-15).

The men in this parable were not only given differing sums of money; those sums were apportioned according to their ability. Students do not come to a classroom with equal abilities. Some have high levels of intelligence; some have well-developed skills. Some have had to struggle to get there at all. Others have loafed their way through high school and yet do well in college.

Teachers know that many C students often have worked harder for their grades than have some of the A students. Yet they cannot switch those grades around, unfair as they may seem. Yet in Jesus' parable even the one who received the smallest sum was still held responsible. If he had invested his one thousand responsibly, he too would have had a reward.

God calls us to make the best possible use of the abilities and talents that we have been given. God will help us do so.

 Lord, help me to use my talents, many or few, responsibly.

Think over your grades. Do they agree with your evaluation of the level of abilities God has given you?

■ ENDURANCE

Rev. 3:7-13: "Since you have kept my command to endure patiently, I will also keep you from the hour of trial" (v. 10).

One does not need to be a valiant hero to endure. One simply needs to hang in there, to dig one's heels in and refuse to be moved. Often we may feel that is all we can do. Others may ridicule our faith, but we hold on against opposition. Others undermine our efforts, but we hold fast. Others try to tempt us into acts of which we disapprove, but we remain true to our own standards. We refuse to let ourselves be compromised. We endure.

Then, having endured, we trust that the promise that we be kept safe from the time of trouble will also endure. We realize that even our enduring is a result of the grace with which God surrounds us. Both the strength to endure and the safety in time of trouble are God's gifts.

 Grant me, O Lord, the strength I need when all I can do is simply to endure.

Think back on an occasion when you realized you had strength to endure what seemed a threat, and thank God for the help you received.

◼ NO TURNING BACK

Luke 9:57-62: "No one who puts his hand to the plow and looks back is fit for service in the kingdom of God" (v. 62).

I have often admired the straight field rows that demonstrate a farmer's skill with a tractor. Heading off into the distance, with seemingly no guide to follow, a farmer plants rows of potatoes or corn that are as straight as a carpenter's rule. That would never happen if the farmer spent the time while driving the tractor looking backward.

Jesus spoke of those who said they wanted to follow him *but*. . . . Perhaps we, too, have had problems with our resolutions to follow him *but*. . . . We may cling to things from our past, things that weaken our commitment to what is ahead. Jesus' reply to those who wanted to take care of what probably seemed like strong priorities may sound harsh, but he was calling for a commitment that was total, unswerving, and as ruler-straight as those field rows.

 Lord, strengthen my commitment to follow you.

Try writing a brief spiritual autobiography. What does it tell you about your spiritual path?

■ IMMEDIATE GRATIFICATION

Gen. 25:29-34: "[Esau] ate and drank, and then got up and left. So Esau despised his birthright" (v. 34).

I worked my way through college partly by clearing the trays brought back at the end of cafeteria meals. The food that we wasted would have fed many families each meal of the day. From what I see today the problem still exists.

We refer to some food-related problems today as eating disorders, anorexia and bulimia, especially common among women. Some counselors estimate that as many as 25% of college women are experiencing these disorders, either starving themselves, or gorging themselves and then abusing themselves to rid their bodies of food already eaten. If you know of someone who exhibits these symptoms, you may do her a real service by encouraging her to take advantage of your campus counseling service.

For Esau, to secure food immediately was an obsession. Even the birthright of the firstborn son meant nothing in comparison to that bowl of lentil stew. For us, too, food can become an obsession or something we misuse or waste. Food is a gift of a loving God—something for us to enjoy, use wisely, and share generously.

 Lord, help me to use food wisely and gratefully.

Think about your own use of food. Are you putting to use what you know about good nutrition?

■ LIFE TOGETHER

Gal. 6:1-5: "Carry each other's burdens, and in this way you will fulfill the law of Christ" (v. 2).

Campus complaints often include such phrases as: "I can't get any studying done in my room because my roommate always has about six people in." "I'm getting tired of putting my roommate to bed when he comes in drunk." "My roommate and I have such different tastes in music—and friends."

At home many American young people are used to having their own rooms and privacy. Then in a usually small dormitory room, two people must accommodate themselves and all that two family cars, perhaps even a U-Haul, can contain. How amazing that the arrangement so often works—in spite of blaring stereos, different waking and sleeping schedules, and varying regulations about who entertains whom where. And in the process we may learn valuable lessons about living with others.

 Lord, help me to live with others in this college community in such a way that we can carry each other's burdens.

Ask your roommate if there is anything you can do to make your life together more cooperative and enjoyable.

■ SO YOU'RE YOUNG

1 Tim. 4:6-16: "Don't let anyone look down on you because you are young, but set an example for the believers" (v. 12).

Students often use their Freshman English themes to talk about their Christian faith. They are asked to write about what is important in their lives, and they may say that the main thing is their faith in Jesus Christ. They are asked about some of the main influences in their lives, and they write about Christian parents or a Christian friend.

If you have made such a witness with your words, how important it is that you back it up with your life! A student who writes about how Jesus Christ is Lord and then skips classes and does sloppy work is not demonstrating the kind of responsible attitude that is consistent with Christian faith.

Some professors have had little personal contact with Christianity, and they may respond to your written witness with hostility, believing you are preaching at them. Don't worry about it. Just make sure that your tone is positive and helpful, and let the Holy Spirit take it from there. The Spirit can do great things.

 Lord, may a part of my academic life here be a witness to those who teach me and those who learn with me.

Begin today to make a habit of praying for each of your professors.

■ MEASURING UP

Gen. 40:1-28: "This is what their father said . . .
giving each the blessing appropriate to him" (v. 27).

Most students are keenly aware of the expectations
their parents have for them. Some of these
expectations are stimulating; others can be frightening.

As his family of sons increased, Jacob must have
pondered what each one would turn out to be—
especially Joseph and Benjamin, sons of his beloved
Rachel. Chapter 49 of Genesis offers an apt description
of the character of each of Jacob's sons.

It can be a great joy to fulfill, or even to surpass,
the expectations of those who love us. Not all of these
expectations, however, may be pleasing to God or
reflect our real abilities and interests. Many students
go through times of tension when their life direction
begins to depart from the hopes and dreams of their
families. At times like these it is important to keep the
lines of communication open—with God, with career
counselors, with campus ministry staff, and with our
families.

 Lord, help me find a career path that is
pleasing to you and right for me.

**Write a letter to your parents in which you "think out
loud" about your life direction.**

■ CHRISTIAN FRIENDS

2 Tim. 2:22—3:5:   "Pursue righteousness, faith, love and peace, along with those who call on the Lord out of a pure heart" (v. 22).

When students first come to college, they are sometimes convinced that their best friends will always be those they knew in high school. That is natural, and those friends should be cherished. Often, however, friendships that develop out of the interests and choices of college turn out to be more enduring.

Friendships made at Christian colleges or through campus ministry are likely to be especially precious and lasting. There is the fellowship of the Christian family at its finest. Out of that community come letters that preserve friendships for decades, reunion weekends that bring great joy, and happy marriages. This is the strengthening friendship of those who love not only us, but also our Lord.

 Lord, let me be the kind of Christian friend to someone else that my best Christian friend has been to me.

Take some time today to reach out to a person in whom you sense the potential of real Christian friendship.

■ THE EXTRAVAGANCE OF LOVE

Luke 15:11-24: "For this son of mine was dead and is alive again; he was lost and is found" (v. 24).

I remember being in a Bible study class in which the leader asked for a definition of the word *prodigal*. Definitions came easily: "a runaway," "one who leaves home," "someone who disappoints his parents," "a rebel," "a juvenile delinquent." The leader was not satisfied with our instant responses. "What does 'prodigal' really mean?" she asked again, "and to whom in the story does it really refer?"

It took a while before someone volunteered the definition "extravagant," and a bit more discussion before someone volunteered the observation she was looking for that the father and the son are both extravagant. When the prodigality of the son has brought him home penniless and disgraced and tattered, he is met by the prodigality of the father, extravagant with his love and compassion.

The extravagant forgiveness of God meets us too even when we do not see ourselves as worthy of it. The most breathtaking extravagance in the story is that of the Father's love.

 Thank you, Father, for the great extravagance of your love for me.

How might you share God's extravagant love with someone who has offended you in the past?

■ USE AND MISUSE

Exod. 20:1-21: "You shall not misuse the name of the Lord your God . . ." (v. 7).

In Old Testament times, respect for God was closely associated with God's name. Each nation had its own gods, and the names of these gods in and of themselves were thought to hold great power.

The corridors and gathering places of colleges are often scenes of misuse of the name of God. The use of God's name in cursing gives others the impression that God has no power and is of no importance to us. As Christians, we need to be on guard against picking up this kind of misuse from the speech of those around us.

Much more serious, however, is a different way in which we misuse God's name. The names of God and of Jesus have been given to us so that we may call on them in prayer, praise, and thanksgiving. The greatest possible offense against God's commandment is when we do not accept the invitation to use those names when we have need for God in our lives.

 Guard my lips, O Lord, and keep me ever dependent on your love and forgiveness.

Make a conscious attempt to avoid the misuse of God's name. Think of alternate phrases that you can use to express surprise or anger.

■ RESEMBLING PETER

Luke 22:54-62: "Then seizing him, they led him away and took him into the house of the high priest. Peter followed at a distance" (v. 54).

Following Jesus at a distance is risky business. When we lose touch with the Master, we also find it easier to ignore or deny him. Just as Peter became alarmed when he was challenged by a servant girl in the courtyard, we know what it is like to resist being publicly identified with Jesus. We have all at some time or other denied him.

Fortunately for Peter and for us, Jesus does not give up on sinful and disobedient human beings. He forgave Peter and made him one of the most important leaders of the early Christian church. Yet it's worth noting how often the figure of the bumbling, stumbling Peter appears in the gospels. It's almost as if God wants to remind us to rely on the power of Christ in our discipleship, not on human courage or commitment.

How marvelous it is that even when we have failed to acknowledge Jesus as our Lord, God calls us back and claims us once again!

 Lord, give me the courage to be faithful to you, in public and in private.

How can you follow Jesus more closely this week?

■ BORN AGAIN

John 3:1-9: "Unless a man is born again, he cannot see the kingdom of God" (v. 3).

He's a born-again Christian," she told me. Perhaps she would have been surprised if I had asked her, "Is there any other kind?" She may have meant that this person could point to a specific day and hour during which an experience of conversion happened. But that isn't the way that everyone is born again.

According to Jesus, a Christian is someone who has been "born again" by water and the Spirit (v. 5). Many Christians have been born again through the work of the Spirit in their lives and through Baptism, and yet cannot pinpoint a particular time in their lives when this happened. It may have been a very gradual process by which they came to personally trust in Christ.

People communicate best when the words they use are precise and accurate. A catch-phrase such as "born-again Christian" may be popular today, but it may not communicate what we really mean to say. We would be better off using the word *Christian* to mean one who is living in a faith relationship with Christ.

 God, help me to live out the new life that you have given me.

What religious labels do you put on others? Are they accurate? Are they helpful?

■ PLAIN HONESTY

Exod. 32:15-24: "Then they gave me the gold, and I threw it into the fire, and out came this calf!" (v. 24).

I wonder where the term "plain honesty" sprang from. Certainly not Aaron! He probably served up his lie to his brother Moses almost without thinking. Moses doesn't dignify it with a reply; it was a blatant lie.

Aaron seems to have some descendants today in classrooms, dormitories, and even faculty offices. The polls give some frightening evidence that we do not look upon cheating, stealing, or lying as being very serious, even if they are direct violations of God's commands. What a raft of rationalizations and more lies they lead to! Some students cheat on tests for some faculty whose lectures may contain whole paragraphs of plagiarism.

We wouldn't want to be treated by doctors who cheated their way through exams on surgical practices or represented by lawyers who cheated their way through law courses. Plain honesty isn't always plain, but it is crucial for a Christian.

 Lord, give me the conscience and courage to be honest.

Have you been dishonest with someone recently? How could you make things right with that person?

■ BREAKING THE STEREOTYPES

John 3:11-21:   "For God did not send his Son into the world to condemn the world, but to save the world through him" (v. 17).

Growing up as I did in a small town, I came to know the word *atheism* but did not know any professed atheists. Attending a church college kept me at a "safe" distance from them, at least as far as I knew. Graduate school was different. There may be no atheists in foxholes (a doubtful cliche), but they were present in some of my literature classes.

I had to adjust myself to the reality that some atheists were likeable, morally admirable people— people whose concern for society and the individuals in it was just as great as that of many Christians I knew. The same was often true for those who called themselves agnostics, though they usually seemed a little less dogmatic or contentious about their beliefs— or lack of them. Some of both varieties became my friends.

Those experiences were good reminders that Christians are not just "nice people," more moral than others. Christians are those who have come into a faith relationship with Christ, and no matter how "nice" or moral they may be, they will never be the same again.

 Lord, teach me to listen to and learn from non-Christians so that I may be a more caring and informed witness to you.

If you know someone who professes to be an atheist, look for a tactful way to tell him or her how much your faith means to you.

■ LIVING IN FREEDOM

John 8:31-38: "So if the Son sets you free, you will be free indeed" (v. 36).

Fear and uncertainty are often experienced by students today. There are many different kinds of fears: fear of failure in one's studies, of not being liked by other students, of choosing the wrong major or career, of running out of money, of not finding a job after graduation.

Jesus said that he can make us "free indeed." We can be freed from the paralysis that comes when fear dominates our lives. There are many good reasons to be concerned about the future, and it is important to make plans. But Jesus has freed us from the burden of always making the "right" choice, of always being the "best," of never making a mistake.

There is a difference between making responsible Christian decisions and avoiding any decision at all out of fear that we might be wrong. In many situations there are a variety of choices that would be consistent with God's will. And the only way we can learn and grow is to give one of those positive choices a try. We will make mistakes and sometimes we will fail, but we will be living out of the freedom Christ has given us.

 Dear Lord, help me to walk in the freedom you have given me.

What fears do you personally find most troubling? Are they fears from which the Son can set you free?

■ RIPE FOR HARVEST

John 4:34-38: "Open your eyes and look at the fields! They are ripe for harvest" (v. 35).

One of the important decisions college students face is the choice of a career. The acceleration of change in today's job market suggests that most people will have several different vocations during their lifetimes. It will be increasingly important to have a liberal education as well as specific skills.

As a Christian, one other concern should also be part of your career planning: "How will I relate my Christian faith to my day-to-day work?" Most of us do not work as full-time paid church professionals. Yet most of the ministry that is done by the church is done by believers who live out their faith commitments in daily life.

As you assess your own abilities and aptitudes and attempt to match them with a vocation, take time as well to prepare yourself for your own personal Christian ministry. You may be called into full-time, paid service in the church. If so, consider that calling seriously. But at least make sure that you have a solid foundation in prayer, Bible study, Christian teaching, and volunteer service. You are Christ's body in the world, and that is your most important vocation.

 Lord, help me to minister to the needs of those with whom I live.

Sign up for a class that will give you an overview of Scripture or train you to minister to the needs of others.

■ ONLY RENTERS

Deut. 20:19: "Are the trees of the field men, that you should besiege them?"

One frequently reads or hears that the exploitation of the earth and the environment is the result of the biblical charge to fill the earth and subdue it. One cannot deny that God gave human beings a very special position in relation to the earth, but a closer reading of the Scriptures shows that exploitation and destruction of the environment is not what God had in mind.

In Deuteronomy 19, God commanded the people of Israel to protect the trees of a city when they were making war against it. Even in wartime, nature was to be protected. The living things that God had given for human sustenance were to be treated with respect and care.

The book of Leviticus reminds us that God is the owner of the earth. Human beings are only stewards (25:18-23). We need to have a clearly reasoned view of our stewardship over the earth. When we destroy the fragile ecosystem that God has established, we not only ruin God's precious gifts, but also undermine our own survival on the earth.

 Lord, I recognize your title to all that our economic system claims belongs to me.

For insurance purposes, it is good to have a list of what you own. Make one out, heading it "Recognizing God's goodness, I have stewardship over the following:"

■ SAFELY ALL THE WAY

Deut. 1:29-33: "You saw how the Lord your God carried you, as a father carries his son, all the way you went until you reached this place" (v. 31).

There are times when we feel our strength is equal to everything demanded of us, and at other times it seems to have drained completely away. Nothing will go right for us. Our grades don't satisfy us; our friends slight us; everything costs more than we had expected; the weather is one bleak, cloudy day after another. We sink into a slough of depression, and others, seeing our somber expressions, avoid us.

Depression is no stranger to the campus. Academic and social pressures are around us. Loneliness often aggravates our moodiness. Families are not near us—or sometimes are part of the problem.

One of the poorest therapies for depression is retreating inside ourselves. Much better to seek out an understanding friend, a campus pastor, or a counselor. Much better to get out of our rooms, go to a concert or a play, even just study among others at the library rather than by ourselves. And we can treasure the words of today's verse and know that they apply to us.

 Lord, thank you for bringing me safely to this place and time.

Memorize the verse for today. Keep a copy on a card where you will come across it often.

■ INDEPENDENCE

1 Peter 2:13-25: "Live as free men, but do not use your freedom as a cover-up for evil; live as servants of God" (v. 16).

It is not always easy for college students to give up the security of and even dependency on home and family. In some ways dependency is easy and comforting. We are taken care of; painful decisions are made for us. Our needs are satisfied. Most of us like independence, but at times we would gladly give it up if someone would be near us, take care of us, be our resource.

One of the positive benefits of time spent away at school is that there is a mix of dependence and independence. There is greater distance from one's family and therefore more opportunity to make one's own decisions and take responsibility for one's actions. At the same time, the college environment often offers a certain amount of structure and support before we enter the working world.

Christians have been given great freedom by God, but they have also been given great responsibility. We are challenged to "stretch our wings" in freedom and yet maintain our dependence on our Creator.

 Father, help me to handle my independence responsibly.

List some of the freedoms and responsibilities that God has given you.

■ THE TRUTH THAT FREES

John 8:25-32: "You will know the truth, and the truth will set you free" (v. 32).

The history of the human race could be told as the process of the unshackling of individuals and societies from bonds forged by ignorance and misunderstanding. Illness and accidents, once thought the work of demons or vindictive enemies, are now recognized as the work of viruses or human action. We no longer believe in deformities as the work of evil spirits—or poverty as always the result of laziness. When we come to know the truth, there is a new freedom from fear and from the need to blame ourselves or others.

Jesus knew that the freeing power of truth applied not only to the physical or psychological, but also to the spiritual. In him the seeker can find not only truth but also the way to it and life in it.

The college experience should be an exciting search for the truth. With that search should come freedom from superstition, falsehood, ignorance, and fear. With it should also come an experiential awareness that the search ends most satisfyingly in the person of Jesus Christ, God's Son. Who could have more access to the truth than the One through whom all things came into being?

 God of all truth, help me to remember that you are the ultimate source of truth.

Use your Bible concordance to find what else Scripture has to say about truth.

■ CHOSEN BY GOD

John 15:8-17: "You did not choose me, but I chose you to go and bear fruit—fruit that will last" (v. 16).

Often our service to our Lord is something we see as happening in the future. When we are children, we think we will really experience life when we "get big." When we are in junior high or middle school, we believe life will really happen when we are in senior high. In senior high we look forward to really living when we get to college—and in college we anticipate real engagement in life when we find our first job and begin to support ourselves.

At every stage, our accomplishments seem postponed until the future, until we have lived almost a fourth of our lives in some yet-to-come existence instead of right now, today.

Life and serving and fruit-bearing belong to our whole life span, not only to a partial period in it. And the fruit we bear as Christians is as important in young adulthood and college as it is later.

 God, may my whole life, now as well as later, bear fruit that will glorify you.

Are there opportunities for service in your life now that you are unnecessarily postponing?

■ THAT LONELY BIRD

Ps. 102:1-12:   "I have become like a bird alone on a housetop" (v. 7).

One might suspect that students who daily mingle with hundreds of others would have little inclination to feel lonely. Yet loneliness is an often-present problem that plagues some people for life. And it occurs in the crowd as often as in the privacy of a dormitory room.

How are you handling loneliness? Do you hide out from others to nurse the feeling? Do you stay home from a social event rather than go alone? Do you take your tray to an empty table in the cafeteria rather than join others who are not intimate friends? If you haven't answered yes to at least one of those questions, you are unusual. Most of us have more of a struggle with loneliness than we would admit to others. It is often tied up with worry about our own worth or acceptability to others.

The writer of our psalm had a problem with loneliness. He related symptoms of fever, lost appetite, insomnia, and tears. But he knew whom to tell about his loneliness. He had faith in the one who would stay with him through the experience, who would hear his cries for help.

 Loving Lord, in my loneliness be my close companion.

Keep your eyes open for someone else who seems as lonely as you sometimes feel. Do something to help to change that person's mood.

■ GIVING AN ANSWER

1 Peter 3:13-22: "Be prepared to give an answer to
everyone who asks you to give the reason for the
hope that you have" (v. 15).

Not all religions have the same emphasis on
evangelism that Christianity does. For example,
Judaism, the religion of Jesus' people, is not a
missionary religion. Even today, a Gentile who
expresses a wish to convert to Judaism is often
discouraged from doing so by a rabbi.

Christians, however, are called to share their faith
with others. The most effective kind of evangelism is
not the sort of "proselytizing" that has received such a
bad name on many college campuses, but rather a
committed and joy-filled Christian life that is backed
up with a clear confession of Jesus as Lord.

There are those who say Christianity is a private,
personal matter about which we need not speak.
Biblical writers knew nothing of this. They lived out
Jesus' command to spread the gospel to all nations
(Matt. 28:18-20).

Evangelism is not only the business of professional
evangelists. Each of us can be a powerful witness for
Christ simply by ministering to those around us as
though they were the Lord himself (Matt. 25:40).

 Lord, help me to share the hope you have
given me.

How might your behavior toward the people in your
life change if you saw Christ in each of them?

47

■ CHANGING MAJORS

Acts 9:1-12: "Get up and go into the city, and you will be told what you must do" (v. 6).

The apostle Paul was a student who changed his major. Living in Jerusalem and studying with the famous Jewish scholar Gamaliel, Paul expended great energy in an attempt to eradicate the followers of Christ. But then he was confronted by Christ on the road to Damascus, and afterward he was never the same. He became the "apostle to the Gentiles" and was instrumental in making Christianity a world religion.

Change in vocation is common on campuses, as is the presence of a large percentage of older students who bring with them an enriching variety of experience, successes, and failures. These experienced students are as valuable as a whole library of vocational information. Younger students might explore these resources by asking questions such as: How did you choose? Why are you changing? What worked for you? What didn't work?

We are never told that Paul came back to finish his study with Gamaliel. He went on to a period of independent study in the wilderness and then some consultations with other church leaders. Sometimes it's important for students to get off one track and onto another. Often these changes bring rich rewards.

 Lord, guide me through the decisions about my life work.

Ask an older student to share a few of his or her life experiences with you.

■ SPEAKING IN SUCH A WAY

Acts 14:1-12: "Paul and Barnabas. . . spoke so effectively that a great number of Jews and Gentiles believed" (v. 1).

Have you taken a speech course? I hope you will. Every believer has a responsibility to bear witness to the faith, and students are often in positions that open up to verbal witness (as well as the witness of our lives).

When Luke wrote that Paul and Barnabas "spoke so effectively that a great number . . . believed," he no doubt meant more than fluency with language. He was referring to their experience of faith and the guidance of the Holy Spirit. But they were also using the abilities they had developed in communicating.

Many students have recognized the value of these abilities, and by practice and experience have made themselves effective communicators. They are ready to witness and assume leadership in both church and public life. Like Paul and Barnabas, they speak in such a way that they attract others to their Lord.

 Lord, help me to develop into an effective communicator so that I make sense when I talk about you.

Check your college bulletin to find a speech course that you can fit into your schedule.

■ THE GIFT OF FORGIVENESS

Eph. 4:25-32: "Be kind and compassionate to one another, forgiving each other, just as in Christ God forgave you" (v. 32).

Living as close together as college students do, interacting as much as dormitory living and crowded classrooms demand, competing for grades that seem so important with students equally bright and alert—all these put heavy demands on our ability to forgive, and sometimes on our ability to ask forgiveness. We need to be adept and sincere both at forgiving and being forgiven. Both may demand courage.

It is sad how little offenses and small grudges add up until things that began as trivial slights swell into major angers and even imagined insults. If we cherish them all, how many friendships melt away into the dark! How much that could have been treasured is lost by graduation time!

Along with forgiving goes the need for both the offender and the one wronged to forget the offense. We cannot do it alone, but God will help us.

 Lord, make me an instant forgiver.

In your contacts with others today, keep alert to your need both to be forgiving and to make peace with someone you may have offended.

■ EYE FOR EYE

Matt. 5:38-42: "You have heard that it was said, 'Eye for eye, and tooth for tooth' " (v. 38).

The law that Jesus quoted in the verse above is commonly looked upon as harsh, unChristian, objectionable—and so it is today. At the time in which that became part of the Old Testament law, however, it was clearly an advance over the primitive law by which humans had lived. Now revenge was to be *limited* to no more than the original offense, a significant step forward.

Those of us who rule out the use of revenge in our lives may be shocked to find how many of those with whom we mingle find the verse from Deuteronomy to which Jesus refers perfectly acceptable for their lives.

This is one example of the fact that we cannot assume that the attitudes Jesus taught will be those of the campus world around us. Even we as Christians often fall far short of the mark. We will find other issues and standards of behavior in which our loyalty to our beliefs will call for us to recognize that we must be different. We are called by our Lord to be different.

Lord, give me courage and love enough so that I dare to follow your ways.

In your conversation with other students today, sample opinions about whether seeking revenge is right. What do you find?

■ ABSOLUTE OR RELATIVE?

Rom. 12:1-2: "Do not conform any longer to the pattern of this world . . ." (v. 2).

Many aspects of life operate relatively. *Hot* may be the 94° of a hot day or the 2000° of a hot engine. *Educated* may mean having a high school diploma or a doctorate in philosophy. There are, certainly, moral decisions in which one must choose between two degrees of good or among a variety of degrees of evil.

Nevertheless, we recognize as believers that God does not waffle in his moral law. Respect for life is not an option we choose but a clearly established command of God. Hatred carries with it its own penalties, whether it is moderate hatred or a burning one. Love is the touchstone in our decisions about matters that are relative, but where God has established absolutes he calls on us to recognize their validity. He also promises us the strength to live by them and forgiveness when we fail.

 Lord, help me not to make mush out of my ethical life by pretending I have the right to change your absolutes to relatives.

Discuss with a friend what you believe are one or two absolute commands from God.

■ OPEN-MINDEDNESS

Acts 17:10-15:   "They received the message with great eagerness and examined the Scriptures every day to see if what Paul said was true" (v. 11).

One of the fruits of a good education should be the open-mindedness demonstrated by the Bereans in this text. They had a willingness to hear coupled with a desire to test what they heard against dependable authority. One of the most admirable kinds of student on any college campus is the one eager to get to the bottom of things, the one not satisfied until there has been exploration of every issue involved, one insistent on finding precise truth. That was the kind of Christian found in the Berean congregation.

Many people come through youth to adulthood bogged down in a quagmire of unexamined opinions and attitudes. They never develop great strength in their beliefs because they have never really questioned them and understood the basis for them. We need to be more like the Berean Christians, who searched for a biblical foundation for what they believed. No academic degree can take the place of that search. The Bible assures us that God is interested in our search for truth and will help us to find it.

 Lord of all truth, give me mental firmness, consistency, and the desire to know the basis for my beliefs.

Talk with your minister about the belief that you find hardest to understand or accept in the Christian faith.

■ ONE GENERATION AWAY

Judg. 2:6-10:   "After that whole generation had been gathered to their fathers, another generation grew up, who knew neither the Lord nor what he had done" (v. 10).

The church," someone has said, "is never more than one generation away from extinction." That is true for the church on campus as well. We can all be thankful for the Christians who faithfully shared the faith from one generation to the next, from the time of Jesus right down to our own day. Even the Scriptures were preserved for us only because monks carefully copied handwritten manuscripts for more than a thousand years.

It's humbling to realize how dependent we are on the work of those who have gone before us, both in terms of our faith as Christians and as students. We need to be reminded that future generations of Christians are equally dependent on what *we* do to share our faith and build on the educational foundations we have been given.

You are a living reminder to others on your campus of all the great things God has done. Others will see the gospel most clearly when it is incarnated in you.

 Dear God, empower my witness to the world as you live and work in me.

Use a mealtime as an opportunity to talk with a friend about what your faith means to you.

■ THAT GREEN-EYED MONSTER

1 Sam. 20:42: "We have sworn friendship with each other in the name of the Lord."

The young David and his friend Jonathan, son of King Saul, had a difficult time because of Saul's jealousy of David. Friendships are precious ingredients of life, as David and Jonathan knew. And when friendships are infected by jealousy, they are put under great strain. Because people on a campus live in such close proximity to each other, jealousy can often be a problem. Some can become fiercely possessive of a friend or roommate, not wanting to share him or her with others. The result may be painful when the friend tries to break free into a more open and satisfying kind of friendship.

Loyalty and love in a friendship are gifts from God to be cherished. But to love and be loyal to a friend does not mean letting someone possess and cling to us in an unhealthy way. It means rejoicing in the companionship and affection which friendship produces, and thanking God for all that friendship adds to life.

 Lord, help me to keep my friendships healthy and loyal, but without being bound by possessiveness.

Arrange to do something enjoyable with a new friend.

■ EVIL, A REALITY

Rom. 1:28-32: "They invent ways of doing evil" (v. 30).

Paul's complaint against some in his day was serious: they were always coming up with more ways to do evil. Many people today look at evil as no more serious than mischief.

The whole idea of evil is one that some would like to relegate to a superstitious past. "Let us who are modern," they say, "realize that what used to be called evil is really just maladjusted, or mistaken, or unwise." It is easy to listen to them; they sound so much more comfortable and compassionate than Paul does in our text.

A belief in the reality of evil should not be difficult for a century that has known the holocaust and the massacres in Cambodia as well as those of Afghanistan and Jonestown. The Bible makes no apology for calling evil what it is—*sin*, first against God, then against others, and also against ourselves. It is also clear in its assurance to us that we can appropriate the victory Jesus' death and resurrection won over evil.

 Lord, help me to be able to face sin as the ugly reality it is and to reject it.

Read a book that describes the holocaust during World War II in Germany. Remember that among those responsible some claimed to be Christians.

■ CHRISTIANS FIRST

Acts 5:27-32:   "We must obey God rather than men!" (v. 29).

"We must obey God rather than men!" Peter declared, facing the pressure of the rulers in Jerusalem to cease his preaching about Jesus. This verse needs to be read side-by-side with Paul's admonition to obey those who are in authority.

Human obedience to authority is one of those murky areas where clear answers are sometimes hard to find, and individual cases may make generalizations unworkable. Christians have a real challenge in this area: they have a responsibility to both a heavenly ruler and to an earthly ruler. One need not look far to find evidence that human laws and actions often disagree with God's commands and intentions.

The example of the apostles given in Acts 4–5 does not give us license to disobey the law out of our own personal convenience. Rather it suggests that there may be times when the demands of Christian morality or discipleship demand a *higher* standard than does the government. There may be times when this higher standard is in direct conflict with a human law. We are Christians first and citizens second. If there is a conflict between our faith and the law, surely it is good citizenship to work for change so that our laws are moral as well as legal.

 Lord, help me always to put your will first in my life.

Read about Dietrich Bonhoeffer's struggle between his Christian beliefs and the need to resist Adolf Hitler.

■ THE SETTLED MIND

Deut. 4:25-31: "If from there you seek the Lord your God you will find him if you look for him with all your heart and with all your soul" (v. 29).

We have a great fear in our day of coming across as too firmly decisive or dogmatic. We cushion what we say with expressions such as "maybe" or "perhaps," which are not meant to be conditionals but to alert our listeners that we are not trying to force our ideas on them.

We need, though, to remember that there are times for firm decisiveness, for recognizing that there are areas of life where we need to be able to make up our minds and hold onto our positions once we have chosen them. These decisions have to do with our Christian beliefs, our ethical standards, and our relations to others on campus.

Going limping between two sides seldom leads to a stable personality. In today's text, Moses claims that those who seek God single-heartedly will be the ones to find him.

 Lord, grant me single-mindedness in serving you and others.

What issue in your life right now do you find hardest to be decisive about? Why is that issue most difficult?

■ BUILDING OUR CHARACTERS

1 Kings 1:5-8: "His father had never interfered with him by asking, 'Why do you behave as you do?' " (v. 6).

I have heard students say, "I am glad my parents loved me enough to discipline me." I doubt they always felt that way when they were in high school and wanted to do everything the crowd did. But added maturity gave insight and appreciation for what had helped them shape their characters. Character does not just happen; it is built and shaped by every decision we make.

Sometimes we see instances of parents who are too busy to discipline their children. One of the most significant verses in the Bible about David as a father of sons is the one above: David had never reprimanded Adonijah about anything. Maybe that was Absalom's problem too—a competitive, frantic life at court for the king's sons, and no guidance, no restraint from a busy father.

The Holy Spirit wants to give us the inner discipline that we need, to shape us continually into what God wants us to be. Sanctification is a lifelong process resulting from God's love for us.

 Lord, continue to shape and discipline me in love.

Spend some time thinking about what aspects of your life still need shaping, and spend some time praying for that to happen.

■ A TIME TO LAUGH

Eccles. 3:1-8: ". . . a time to weep and a time to laugh" (v. 4).

The Bible is filled with laughter. God laughed. Abraham laughed, as did his wife Sarah. The wicked laugh. There are those who laugh who shall weep, and those who weep who shall soon laugh. Some of the laughter is derisive; other laughter is full of joy. Jesus was never portrayed as laughing, but there is often humor behind his words.

Many places on campus provide an opportunity to study laughter. Some students are natural comedians and need only raise an eyebrow to have their companions in shouts of merriment.

Laughter may be joyous or cruel, fun or hurtful. It runs the entire gamut, and the tone of it tells much about its purpose. What you laugh at reveals much about you, just as someone's never laughing tells much about him, or someone's inability to handle being laughed at reveals something about her. Merry laughter at something genuinely funny is a gift of God to the laugher and from the laugher to all around him. God who permits sorrow also restores laughter to us.

 Lord, grant my friends and me the gift of kind, merry laughter all our days.

Take time to do some analysis of the laughter around you for a day. What do you learn about its motivation?

■ ENCOURAGEMENT

Rom. 15:1-9: ". . . that through endurance and the encouragement of the Scriptures we might have hope" (v. 4).

I just came home from our traditional campus Christmas candlelight service. Our campus pastor talked about what Christmas means—the God who appeared to low-caste shepherds, who was born in the messiness of a stable in order that we might know his love. We can invite God into the messiness of our own lives and find acceptance and peace.

On most campuses there are clergy and lay ministers who offer counseling, teaching, and friendship. Pastors from nearby churches often make themselves available for ministry to students on smaller campuses. These campus ministers are ready to be supportive in our lonely moments and comforting in our griefs, and to listen when we need to talk something out confidentially. We can grow as we learn from their example that being a Christian in the intellectual world is a viable option.

Our campus experience can be richer for their friendship and help, and their ministry can be encouraged by our participation.

 Lord, bless and strengthen those in ministry on my campus.

If you do not already know, take time today to find out about the ministry your church supports on your campus.

■ TO FOLLOW WHOM?

1 Cor. 1:10-17:   "Is Christ divided? Was Paul crucified for you?" (v. 13).

Rather than being flattered that there were those who saw him as their favorite leader, Paul was indignant with those who had chosen sides among the leaders of the congregation in Corinth.

It is easy for us in our maturing to fasten on one popular teacher or spiritual leader who suits our needs and personalities. That person becomes important to our growth, a mentor we honor and respect and love.

There are joys in these relationships, but there may be dangers as well. The veneration can become so strong that students may never go beyond their teacher, even though they have the potential to do so. Or students may become so dependent on their mentors that they cannot function when their mentor is gone.

Our mentor, the one whom we can never follow too closely and who will always be with us, is Christ.

 Lord, may I always be willing to have you be first in my life.

Is someone acting as a mentor in your college life? What are you learning from him or her that you can share in turn with someone else?

■ THE WISEST PRAYER

1 Kings 3:1-15: "So give your servant a discerning heart to govern your people and to distinguish between right and wrong" (v. 9).

We learn almost nothing about who Solomon's teachers were. David was aging by the time Solomon was a young man. Did David spend time with his son teaching him kingcraft? The prophet Nathan showed an interest in Solomon's being his father's successor. Did the prophet watch over the young prince? Solomon was an obedient son of the nation's greatest king. Whoever his teachers, the prince was in many ways a credit to their instruction.

In the dream in which God asked what gift he would like—wealth or wisdom—Solomon chose well. He asked for wisdom with justice and knowledge of the difference between good and evil. What a great prayer for those of us who seek an education on a university or college campus! It is not enough to have facts—raw information. The ability to look at knowledge with understanding and perceptivity makes for wisdom. That wisdom God gives is anchored in justice, and the respect for justice leads us to distinguish good from evil.

 Lord, help me to learn wisdom as well as facts.

What differences have you noticed between people who are the collector-of-facts type and those who handle facts with wisdom and discretion?

■ WHEN BAD NEWS COMES

Job 10:8-17: "You gave me life and showed me kindness, and in your providence watched over my spirit" (v. 12).

People who claim to know all the answers when explaining the tragedies of this life are more than daring; they are foolhardy. Job's comforters thought they had all the answers when they debated with Job, and much of what they said still sounds good to many today who want to wrap God up in their pat answers. Surely they had defended God nobly. Yet, at the end of the story (42:7), God repudiated their help. Not only that, God reproved them, "because you have not spoken of me what is right, as my servant Job has." How that must have knocked them back on their heels!

From time to time we all hear bad news that comes from home, about accidents our friends are involved in, illnesses, or financial crises. Better than handing our friends pat answers, we would do well to make a special effort to spend some time with them, hold them close when they need to cry, and wrap them in our love.

 Lord, help me to trust you without insisting on explaining things I can't understand.

Give a friend who has been having a hard time a reassuring, affectionate call today.

■ INTELLECTUALS

1 Cor. 1:18-25:   "Where is the scholar? Where is the philosopher of this age? Has not God made foolish the wisdom of the world?" (v. 20).

Within the academic world one sometimes gets the impression that Christian faith is considered a sure sign of ignorance or narrow-mindedness, in spite of the fact that some of the most brilliant thinkers in the history of Western civilization believed in God: Augustine, Aquinas, Copernicus, Pascal, Newton, Kant, Kierkegaard—the list goes on and on. And literature has been blessed by the contributions of writers such as Dostoyevski, Lewis, Tolkien, and Flannery O'Connor.

Citing these examples, however, should not obscure the fact that Christianity does contain an offense to the intellect—a stumbling block to our human, rational ways of thinking. The wisdom of the cross is God's wisdom, not a human theory that fits neatly with the observations of physics.

Christian students need not fear to use all the mental capacities God has given them. But they should also remember that the greatest wisdom of all is revealed in the crucifixion and resurrection of Christ.

 Fortify my faith, Lord, and equip my mind, that I may serve you better.

Is there a Christian professor at your college whom you respect highly? Make an effort to become better acquainted with him or her.

■ A SENSIBLE CAUTION

Ps. 27:1-6: "In the day of trouble he will keep me safe in his dwelling" (v. 5).

To the psalm writer, no place seemed as safe as the Temple, the center of Hebrew worship. There God would shelter him and give him security.

Personal safety is a concern in our society today, even on college campuses. While some parts of our country are much safer than others, even campuses in quiet settings have concerns. College women are warned not to walk across campuses alone at night. Even men would rather be with someone else than walk alone through isolated passenger tunnels. Women faculty hesitate to teach evening classes that would mean leaving their cars in dark parking lots.

Prayer for safety is no justification for being careless. God has never promised that we will not run the same risks and dangers others are subject to, but God *has* promised to be with us.

 Lord, keep guard over me in a world that may have unexpected dangers.

Think through your daily routine and try to spot which of your activities might bring you into situations in which you need to exercise caution.

■ AN IMPORTANT DEFINITION

Psalm 8:   "You made him a little lower than the heavenly beings and crowned him with glory and honor" (v. 5).

How human beings define themselves is vitally important to how they live. If they accept Machiavelli's definition of humans as political animals whose welfare depends on their being well-governed, they will make that their first priority. If, in Marxist fashion, they see themselves primarily as economic beings for whom economic equality and well-being is most important, that will dominate. If Freud's teaching that they are primarily sexual beings whose nature will not hear sexual repression is accepted, that definition will determine human behavior.

Psalm 8 poses that vital question, "What is man, that you are mindful of him, the son of man that you care for him?" (v. 4). Looking at the majesty of the heavens, the poet is forced to that question. The answer of the psalm places human beings high in the hierarchy of living things—depending on your translation, either next to God himself or to the angels. It regards them as crowned with glory and honor. How different from the cynicism about human beings evident in much contemporary literature!

We have been given stewardship over creation, the responsibility for other living things. What a compliment!

O Lord, our Lord, help me to have a sense of your indescribable greatness!

What would be your definition of the role God expects educated human beings to act out in relationship to creation?

■ LET SOMEBODY HELP

1 Tim. 1:12-19:   ". . . holding on to faith and a good conscience" (v. 19).

Paul spoke of Timothy as his spiritual son. After Paul had spent as much time as he could allow with the new church at Ephesus, he left Timothy in charge there. Later he wrote a letter to his young protegé, giving him advice about handling the developing congregation and the people in it.

In college, students are also preparing to meet the professional expectations of those in administrative or supervisory positions. It is not always easy to admit our responsibility to those over us. We like the feel of independence in our work, the freedom to plan and to execute our plans.

Timothy gained much from the counsel and supervision of his spiritual father. We can learn much from Paul's words to Timothy in our text. We can also gain much from the counsel and help of our teachers and advisors. They are valuable in helping us to "keep our faith and a clear conscience."

 Help me, Lord, to have an open, healthy attitude toward those who give me professional and spiritual guidance.

Aside from your family members, who has been your most helpful counselor? Find a way to let him or her know you appreciate the help.

■ GOD WILL TEACH YOU

Ps. 32:8-11: "I will instruct you and teach you in the way you should go" (v. 8).

Students often wrestle with decisions about which school to attend in order to receive the best education or the best training in the field they have chosen. It is important to have good professors and facilities.

"I will instruct you and teach you in the way you should go," God assured the psalmist. God desires to be our teacher. There are many different ways God instructs and teaches us: through Scripture, preaching and teaching, through the counsel of friends, through a burden we may feel about a need that we can help to meet.

God expects us to make use of the opportunities we have been given to receive an education, to meet the needs of the world around us, and to look for more results from our life and work than just the highest possible salary. We need to be prayerful and open as we prepare for our vocations. The promise that God will instruct and teach us applies also to us today.

 Father, help me to be open to your teaching in my education and working life.

Ask several friends who seem happy and satisfied in their work what kinds of satisfactions they receive from it.

■ FRUIT OF THE SPIRIT

Gal. 5:19-26:   "But the fruit of the Spirit is love, joy, peace, patience, kindness, goodness, faithfulness, gentleness and self-control" (v. 22).

A campus pastor told me recently that abuse between roommates is one of the problems students most often bring to him. Abuse need not be physical, though it may be. It may instead be derisive speech, ridicule, shunning, one subjecting the other to embarrassing situations, disregard of reasonable privacy, or constant and noisy company.

Living under such conditions may be a good lesson in patience and character building, but it can be hard on one's being a good student. God can provide for those who must remain in a difficult situation, giving patience and strength. But for the sake of your studies, if you have a problem of this kind you may need to find a situation in which the fruit of the Spirit is growing in the hearts of not only one but all who share your room or apartment.

 Lord, may those who live with me see the fruits of the Spirit in me.

If you have a problem related to abuse by another student, talk it over with a counselor.

■ WHAT IS THAT TO YOU?

John 21:15-23: "If I want him to remain alive until I return, what is that to you? You must follow me" (v. 22).

How much of our lives we spend comparing or contrasting ourselves with others, so often seeing their abilities or appearance or possessions as superior to our own! Peter seems to have had the same problem. His pride still smarting from his denial of Jesus, no doubt, he heard Jesus predict an unhappy end of life for him, and his first question was, "What about John?" Surely Peter feared that the Master must have been more satisfied with John.

But John's future was not the issue. What Jesus was concerned about was that the denier become the follower again, that Peter the rock be restored to obedience. "You must follow me."

For us, too, the issue is not how our call to serve Jesus compares to that of Peter or John, Mary or Martha. His call to us is an individual matter, suited to our situation and our abilities, extended to us even if we too have at times been deniers. With the call comes also the grace to undertake it and live it out in the days and years that lie before us.

 Lord Jesus, please make your call to discipleship so unmistakably clear that I cannot help but hear it.

Read John 18:15-18, 25-27 along with John 21:15-23. Place yourself in Peter's shoes as you read the two stories.

■ FRUIT OF THE LIGHT

Eph. 5:1-11:   ". . . for the fruit of the light consists in
all goodness, righteousness and truth" (v. 9).

Light and darkness constantly influence our world.
People live under one or the other of these canopies.
Paul and his readers once lived in darkness, but when
they became believers they came into the light. Now,
energized by the presence of light, they are to bring
forth the harvest that is natural when the light shines
upon the "soil" of their lives—goodness, righteousness,
and truth.

Often in our world we find that goodness is looked
upon as dull, unexciting. When Dickens created his
model of a truly good man, his character was an
illiterate blacksmith. Dostoyevski's model was a man
others looked upon as an idiot. Will the harvest of
goodness in our lives make us suspect in the
intellectual world? Perhaps, but not necessarily. The
light of God producing a harvest in our lives will make
us like Jesus, and nothing is more desirable than that.

 Lord, may your light produce a rich harvest of
goodness in my life.

**What do you see as the most essential characteristics
of goodness? Who that you know is a good
representative of it?**

■ THE CHURCH CHRIST LOVES

Eph. 5:25-30: ". . . Christ loved the church and gave himself up for her" (v. 25).

People sometimes talk about how many problems they have with "the institutional church," which they see as lacking integrity, commitment, enthusiasm, or any number of other things. The institutional church is contrasted with the ideal church Paul described as a structure joined together and growing into a holy temple in the Lord (Eph. 2:19-22).

The church has always had many shortcomings. Even where Christians try to work together, there are problems that need to be overcome. Human sinfulness, pride, and stubbornness afflict the whole Christian church—and always have, even in New Testament times.

Every individual Christian, every Christian organization, and every church institution needs the forgiveness and reconciliation that Christ provides. It is an amazing and wonderful thing that "Christ loved the church and gave himself for it" in spite of our human failings. The whole body of Christ—organized and disorganized—can take hope from that!

 Lord of the church, thank you that you are still working out your plan for the church through us, in spite of ourselves.

Visit a church from another Christian tradition than your own and observe the similarities and differences.

■ UNITY

John 18:20-23: "May they be brought to complete unity to let the world know that you sent me" (v. 23).

As a student you have the chance to explore not only your own ideas but also those of others. For many who have grown up in the activity of a particular congregation and denomination, college brings opportunities to live among people of different denominations and backgrounds. Campus ministry organizations often include people from a variety of Christian traditions.

Even though there are many issues that divide one Christian denomination from another, there is also unity when both confess faith in Christ as Savior and Lord. Jesus himself prayed to the Father for complete unity in the church. He knew that conflict in the church would hinder its witness in the world.

Take advantage of the opportunities you have to find out more about other Christian denominations. But don't forget to find out enough about your own tradition that you can explain its distinctive perspectives to others. The first step toward better cooperation among Christians is learning more about one another.

 Thank you, Lord, for what my Christian heritage does to enrich my faith.

When writing or talking to your parents, ask them to tell you why they have the denominational affiliation they do.

■ HANDLING CHANGE

Ps. 102:18-28: "You remain the same, and your years will never end" (v. 27).

Change in the college years often has to do with some kind of loss. In the progress from high school to college we lose contact with many of our high school friends; we no longer spend as much time with our families; we are not as often at our home church. We may lose jobs and need to find and adjust to new ones. In college we become adjusted to roommates and lose them; we make good friends, and are separated from them when they transfer or graduate. Then *we* graduate, and again there are changes and adjustments to be made.

Most of us handle these losses and changes with an adequate degree of poise. We realize that change is a part of life that will continue to be with us after we leave the campus. But it is a lasting comfort to realize that no matter how demanding the changes, how great the adjustments, our God is a constant. God will never lose interest in us or decide he does not love us any more. Knowing that, we can handle those other losses with God's help.

 Lord, thank you that you are an unchangeable rock.

Take time to write a note or call a high school friend in order to strengthen your friendship.

■ CHRISTIANS UNDER CONSTRUCTION

Phil. 1:3-11: "He who began a good work in you will carry it on to completion until the day of Christ Jesus" (v. 6).

Do we find things about ourselves that trouble and dismay us? A wall plaque says, "Be patient with me. God isn't done with me yet." How important that we believers keep this ever in mind in our relationships with each other!

Most of us have likely had times in our lives when we found it very hard to forgive someone who had offended us. How much better if we could forgive that person knowing that God is still shaping and perfecting us. And if God is satisfied with that, shouldn't we be able to accept it?

The "good work" of God is going on all over our campus—in the dorms and in the food service, in the classes and on the track team. Adults, too, are under construction. So when you see that person who used to bug you in every class you had with him or her, watch for some signs of spiritual reconstruction—in both yourself and in others.

 Lord, please continue work of construction in me.

Is there someone in your life who is still under construction and needs your forgiveness today?

■ YOUR POWERS OF OBSERVATION

Ps. 104:1-24: "How many are your works, O Lord! In wisdom you made them all" (v. 24).

The person who wrote Psalm 104 would have made an excellent teacher for a science course. The wonder of light and the heavens, clouds and wind, oceans and mountains, floods and tides, springs and rain, birds and cattle, wine and olive oil, storks and goats, lions and people—all these captured his attention. As a result, the writer was encouraged to worship.

How observant are you? As you walk to class, have you observed the endless variety of shapes of leaves, the designs of the insects that flit around you, the mosses that flourish at the base of trees? How about your observation of others? Do you enjoy the variety in their appearance? Do you notice when another student's face reveals loneliness or grief? Do you see the signs of shyness or of depression? We who have eyes, let us see.

 Lord, help me learn to be more observant.

Take a walk around a block or two and keep your eyes open for something you have never seen before.

■ THAT BIG DECISION

1 Cor. 7:1-17: "I wish that all men were as I am. But each man has his own gift from God" (v. 7).

The concerns of students during college years are not all academic. These are also years during which common interests and attractions may lead to romance, strong friendships are formed between men and women, and marriage partners are chosen.

John and Debbie may be planning a wedding soon after graduation. David and Sue, on the other hand, intend to be well launched in their careers before they think of marriage. Or they may plan to remain single. Lisa and Tom would like to marry but they have found no one to whom they are ready to make that kind of commitment.

There is a new freedom in our day to choose between marriage and singleness—a freedom that may remove the pressure to marry early because of societal influence or to marry at all if one chooses singleness. Paul recommended singleness in his turbulent day of persecution. To marry or to remain single is an option to be chosen with the guidance a loving God makes available to us through prayer and careful examination of our willingness to make a lifelong commitment.

 Lord, help me to make the right decisions about marriage or singleness in my life.

Seek out a happily married friend and a single one for a conversation with each about marriage and singleness.

■ MEDDLERS

2 Thess. 3:6-16: "We hear that some people among you are idle. They are not busy; they are busybodies" (v. 11).

People who live in close proximity, as in dormitories and blocks of offices in campus buildings, are naturally tempted to discuss each other and observe each other's lives closely. Curiosity, if nothing else, causes us to examine each other with interest. There is nothing strange about that. Human beings are fascinating and unique, and where interest and a healthy curiosity are the motives, the watcher of people can learn much about life itself.

But where observation turns to gossip and invasion of privacy, the situation turns to what Paul described in his letter to the Thessalonians. How much healthier the campus experiences of the one who can observe and know when to remain silent, who can show interest in a person without interfering where he or she is unwelcome, who can feel affection and friendship that protect rather than violate another person's rights and privacy.

 Lord, help me to keep my eyes open and my mouth shut in the right places.

Develop a habit of tactfully changing the subject when a conversation turns to the practice of busybodying.

■ CALLED TO BE FREE

Gal. 5:13-15: "Serve one another in love" (v. 13).

Sexual abuse, if we are to believe the media, the words of counselors, and workers in shelters for battered people, is frequent in our society. We would like to believe that our efforts toward sexual equality and justice are bearing fruit, but with supposed advances in these areas come increased numbers of cases of rape, so closely related to violence and molestation.

Relationships we have with each other in our society are sometimes puzzling. Why would a woman go out a second time with a man who abused her physically? Is she that afraid he will be the only one to show an interest in her? Why would a man seek the company of a woman who belittles and insults him? Is a sick self-image to blame? Singleness is surely a better alternative than a violent marriage.

God's plan for sexuality and sex is that they be beautiful and meaningful, sanctified by the love that leads us to serve one another gladly and with dignity. God's plan in marriage is still for a man and a woman to be joined in love and committed for life. To that end God will give us strength and grace to treat each other with respect.

 Lord, make violence and hatred so foreign to me that I will never, even in hottest anger, use them against others.

Take a few minutes to think about the most loving, beautiful marriage you have known, and what makes it that way.

■ BEING GOD'S PERSON

Ps. 145:1-13: "I will exalt you, my God the King; I will praise your name for ever and ever" (v. 1).

What a wonderful example of variety is a college student body! Ages from 16 to 70, skin shades from pale through ebony, and differences in disposition, personality, talents, senses of humor, financial status, and beliefs.

God's creation is clear evidence that God loves variety. You are a part of that variety, a unique person of whom, even if you be a twin, there is no duplicate on earth. Why, then, do so many work hard at being duplicates of those about them? Is it sensitivity to being labeled different? Isn't being different an asset—something that should help us win a position or friends? Who needs friends who are carbon copies of each other?

God made you unique. God wants you to be your own person—and his. God wants you to be alert to his approval more than to the pressures to conform to those around you. If you leave yourself open to the guidance of the Holy Spirit, God will make you something very special, something precious, because you are one of a kind—God's kind.

 Lord, make me more concerned about being like you than being like others.

Observe your own behavior today. How much does it change to adapt itself to others? How much to preserve its own uniqueness?

■ LIVING RIGHT NOW

Ps. 119:97-112:   Accept, O Lord, the willing praise of my mouth, and teach me your laws" (v. 108).

It is human nature not to think of instruction as sweet—and sometimes to find it tedious. Some young people, with the gates of high school closed behind them, think the prospect of another four years of study and work ahead of them almost too much to face. "Will I never be done with this business of preparing for life," they say, "and get on with the business of living?"

How important it is in the midst of the pressures that face us to remember that college is not only preparation for life but it *is* life itself—life to be enjoyed and relished at the same time as we study. We do not look forward to making friends only when we get out on the job; we cherish some of the best friendships of our lives right now. We grasp opportunities to practice the development of our talents not only when college is done; we put them to use in local churches and campus ministries right now. Life is now, as well as then, to be lived to the fullness God makes possible.

 Lord, help me not to put life off into some vague future but to live it every day, right now.

Plan to do some special thing this week to be enjoyed for itself now rather than put aside as something to do when college is done.

■ DON'T "X" ME OUT

Philemon 7-16: ". . . no longer as a slave, but . . . as a brother in the Lord" (v. 16).

Onesimus was a slave who had fled from the house of Philemon, Paul's friend, and found his way to Paul's dwelling in Rome. He had become a believer, and now, wanting to make things right with his master, was going, Paul's letter in hand, back to Philemon.

Paul appealed to Philemon to treat Onesimus as a brother in Christ. Tradition tells us that Onesimus later became a bishop in the early church. Paul's appeal must have been granted on behalf of a slave.

Many students on a college campus know what it means to be X-ed out by those who are better looking, more athletic, more well-to-do, more talented, with more sparkling personalities. God could take a runaway slave and make him a bishop. He can take those of us who are X-ed out by others and develop us into fruitful, fulfilled individuals.

 Lord, give me the kind of sensitivity to the worth of others that will keep me from ever X-ing them out, and help me know how to handle my own being X-ed out by others.

Keep your eyes open on campus today for someone others seem to be X-ing out, and be a friend.

■ THE FAMILY OF GOD

Psalm 133:   "How good and pleasant it is when brothers live together in unity!" (v. 1).

It's great to be a part of the family of God—at least a family that gets along together. Being part of a family means sharing the deep, moving experiences of life. One of the unfortunate facts of life away from our families is that we cannot always be home to share many of the cherished experiences of everyday life. An important part of adjusting to campus life is finding a good listener with whom we can share our feelings about such moments.

I remember so vividly the early morning visit of a rather distraught but happy young man whose wife had during the night given birth to their first child. None of their family had been able to be with them. The telephone announcements had been made. Now the young father could begin to key down, but somehow it wouldn't seem real until he could tell someone the whole anxious but marvelous experience. I have never lost the thrill of being the one permitted to share that account. To be invited into the life of another is an experience to treasure and respect, and for which to be grateful.

 Thank you, Lord, for other people with whom to share my life.

Make a deliberate attempt today to be a warm, receptive listener for some other student.

■ BE WILLING TO BE HELPED

James 4:7-10: "Humble yourselves before the Lord, and he will lift you up" (v. 10).

Even though we are in the business of wisdom-getting, we on a campus are not wise enough to be able to meet all our own needs. There are times when we need to make use of those who are trained to help us.

Depression is a common problem among students. We may learn in an introductory psychology class how to handle a mild case of it, but when it is more serious it is time to see a minister, counselor, or a doctor.

If your reading, writing, or math skills do not seem to be serving you well, it is time to seek out the services your college provides to help you improve them.

We like to believe we are competent to handle all our own problems, and with many of them we fare well. But just as we must admit that we can't handle our own spiritual needs without God's help, so we are wise to admit we need the expertise of others in other areas of life as well.

 Lord, help me to seek out the aid I need from you and from others.

Check a map of your campus to locate the counseling center so you will know where to find it if you or some friend of yours should need help from it.

■ THE IGNORED OPPORTUNITY

Rev. 3:14-22: "If anyone hears my voice and opens the door, I will go in and eat with him, and he with me" (v. 20).

Moods on campuses vary with the years. But there is usually a sizable number in a student body who believe they will be misunderstood if they make close friendships with faculty. Many faculty and students thus lose out on what might be rewarding friendships in their fields of study for a lifetime, all because of fear of being misunderstood or misinterpreted by others.

Do we sometimes treat Christ like that, seeking to maintain only a formal, correct relationship, but never allowing the warm, loving relationship he yearns to have with us? Jesus will never misinterpret our desire to come close to him.

 Lord, draw me into a lifelong relationship of love with you.

Stop in to see one of your instructors just to get acquainted and begin to develop a friendly relationship.

■ CYNICISM

Eph. 15:1-4:   ". . . that through endurance and the encouragement of the Scriptures we might have hope" (v. 4).

Cynicism can thrive in an intellectual environment. "That researcher did a great thing for the university and society as a whole," one person might say but someone else's cynical response may be, "He was in it for the money."

There is a big difference between *cynicism* and *realism*. Cynicism sometimes takes root when students see naive and idealistic ideas about the world shaken. They may become disillusioned and bitter. Realism, on the other hand, recognizes the selfish, sinful side of human beings, but does not become blind to the positive aspects of life.

Christian faith gives us a realistic, but not cynical, view of the world. It has no illusions about the character of human beings. Yet faith sees beyond human sin and stubbornness and grasps the great hope of salvation in Christ. Jesus is the solid rock on which we can stand, knowing that he is the author and preserver of every good thing.

Lord, help me avoid both excess idealism and the bitterness of cynicism. Give me a realistic view of life, and faith to grasp the hope you have given me.

Challenge a cynical statement you hear this week with a word of hope.

■ TAMING OUR TONGUES

Prov. 6:12-19: ". . . things the Lord hates . . . a man who stirs up dissension among brothers" (vv. 16, 19).

A magazine that comes to my house had an article that talked about the *worthwhile* aspects of gossip. I could hardly believe my eyes! Of course it did briefly warn of destructive extremes. Robert Frost called gossip our "guessing at each other." Unfortunately, that guessing all too often goes far afield and has deadly effects on the reputations and happiness of others.

I have found three questions helpful in deciding when I should reveal what I know. They are not original with me, but they do give good guidance. First, is it true? That may be less easy to ascertain than we think. If we cannot be sure of that, why speak? Second, is it kind? If the result of its being told will be to bring pain or disgrace, why speak? Third, is it necessary? Perhaps the story is true. Perhaps the motivation is not to bring pain or harm, but if no positive good is served, why tell it?

No wonder the writer of Proverbs said, "When words are many, sin is not absent" (10:19). There are times and situations in which the truth needs to be spoken about others, but these times are far fewer than we like to believe.

 Lord, place a guard on my lips, especially when I talk about others.

Make it a practice not to say negative things about people who are not present.

■ THE PURSUIT OF EXCELLENCE

Phil. 4:4-9: ". . . if anything is excellent or praiseworthy—think about such things" (v. 8).

To keep one's mind filled with what is good and praiseworthy in our day is a mammoth challenge, not only because so much in our media is violent and degrading, but also because so much of it is trivial and cheap. It is difficult to discern that which is truly worthwhile out of the constant barrage of intellectual clutter that bombards our eyes and ears.

One of my finest professors in college frequently said, "You do not have time for the ordinary. You have time only for the good." Granted, we need what is relaxing as well as what is profound, what is simple as well as what is complex. Nevertheless, it is easy to become just a passive observer of commercially packaged fantasy rather than a responsible participant in the joys and challenges of real life.

Our society is rapidly moving toward the kind of vulgar and violent entertainment that was common in the ancient cities of the Roman Empire. St. Paul was being very "contemporary" in advising the Philippians to concentrate on that which was "excellent or praiseworthy."

 Dear God, help me exchange passive and destructive forms of entertainment for experiences that are involving, fun, and excellent.

As you walk around campus today, notice the variety of mind-fillers that are bidding for your attention.

■ YOUR GOOD NAME

Eccles. 7:1-8: "A good name is better than fine
perfume" (v. 1).

The loss of a reputation, a good name, has been a
serious tragedy for many people. They have not
realized its seriousness when they have yielded to the
temptation to steal from a roommate's wallet, to turn
in a plagiarized paper, to become involved with
drugs—or lies, or irresponsible sexual behavior. Then,
to their dismay, they realize they are no longer trusted
with responsibility; their lives become a kind of
probation before others. They may even be asked to
leave college. Discipline on a campus is often handled
quietly, but it may have serious consequences.

Our personal, private name needs to be carefully
treasured. Once it has been tainted, the wrong may be
forgiven, but the consequences may be hard to hide.
It is good to know, however, that through God's
mercy reputations may with time be restored. It may
be our privilege to help someone experience that
restoration.

 Lord, give me grace to treasure my good
name, because my name and yours are linked
together.

**Show some redemptive kindness to someone on
campus who has endangered his or her good name.**

■ HISTORY

Judges 2:10-19: "Another generation grew up who knew neither the Lord nor what he had done for Israel" (v. 10).

Critics of our educational system have complained for several decades that the study of history is being neglected, that a new generation has come to adulthood ignorant of what has shaped us as a nation to what we are today. A frequent complaint against politicians is that they seem to know little about the forces history has set in motion that are now influencing our direction as a nation.

Christian students who want to be equipped to take their part in the coming of God's kingdom need to study history—the working of God in human nations, the interaction of governments with the great forces of God's will for human beings. For us history is not accidental. It is moving in the direction God's will and human decisions are taking us. Looking at what God has done in history can illuminate that direction and help us to follow it.

 Lord, give me clear vision to understand what I read in your acts in history.

Register for a class that surveys the history of Western civilization or American history.

■ PREPARING, NOT CRAMMING

Heb. 12:1-11:   ". . . surrounded by such a great cloud of witnesses" (v. 1).

Like the Hebrews to whom the author of our text wrote, we do our work with a crowd of witnesses about us. Faculty watch our development as majors or minors in their fields of study. Perhaps you are not aware of being discussed as a degree candidate in your field, but you are. Teachers from home high schools compare notes on how former students are doing. Friends and family are more aware of how you are doing than you may think.

The author of Hebrews described the vast company of God's faithful who have through the centuries cheered each other on. That "cloud" of witnesses of the saints of the ages is cheering for us, too, not to make us feel pressured, but to encourage and stimulate us as we run this part of our race of life. It is our privilege to cheer others on as well. A word of hearty congratulations may give new strength to someone in need of encouragement.

 Lord, keep my ears open to those who encourage me and closed to those who would tempt me to do less than my best

Watch for a few minutes the joggers and runners so common around a university campus. What that you observe can be applied to the race about which our text speaks?

■ A SENSE OF WONDER

Prov. 30:15-31: "There are three things that are too amazing for me, four that I do not understand" (v. 18).

The wisdom writers revealed a lively sense of wonder about the world of their day. They knew nature. They marveled at the flight of eagles and watched snakes gliding across rocks. They observed the flight of locusts and the behavior of colonies of ants. And all of these things spoke about God.

People take such pride today in being blasé, in acting as if they know it all, in never allowing themselves to be taken by surprise. How much more satisfying it is to develop our powers of observation, to learn about the world we live in and allow ourselves to be surprised by it! There is a gleam of excitement and the spark of vision in those for whom life has a sense of wonder—a sense which is one of God's gifts to us.

 Thank you, Creator God, for a world that is full of variety and wonder. Help me constantly to grow in my appreciation of it.

Make up a list of your own "four simple things that are too mysterious for me to understand."

■ IN THE BREAKING OF BREAD

Luke 24:28-35: "Then the two told what had happened on the way, and Jesus was recognized by them when he broke the bread" (v. 35).

Most of us have some unique mannerism or feature by which our friends recognize us—a laugh or a sneeze, a pattern of footsteps or a cough. After Jesus' death and resurrection, two of his disciples sought a meal in Emmaus and persuaded their traveling companion to eat with them. It was this man's distinctive way of breaking the bread that identified him, that opened their eyes to his being their Lord. All those seven miles he had walked and talked with them and, submerged in their grief and disappointment, they had not recognized him until they noted that familiar manner of breaking bread.

We, too, come to a deeper recognition of Jesus as our daily companion in life in the breaking of the bread of the Lord's Supper. Whether in our home church or a service on campus, we come with our particular joys or disappointments and go from there warmed and comforted. We are reminded that even in those moments of life in which we do not recognize Christ he has been walking with us all the while.

 Lord, help me to rejoice in and recognize your presence with me.

Have you found in your college setting a congregation where you can participate in the Lord's Supper?

■ LEARNING TO BE SILENT

James 3:1-12: "If anyone is never at fault in what he says, he is a perfect man, able to keep his whole body in check" (v. 2).

How often when people look back at something in their lives for which they feel shame or remorse, that something has to do with what they have *said* to someone—a family member or a friend. Or a roommate. They grew angry when they were reprimanded and shouted an unkind rebuttal. The praise a friend received made them jealous, so they slashed back with a jab designed to bring the other person down to size. Another student reported what someone said about them, and they struck back with a derogatory statement about the speaker. Sometimes we speak the hatred we feel from being hassled, and then later we wish we had held our tongues.

How much of a lifetime it takes to bring the tongue under control! Someone once said, "It takes a human being four or five years to learn to speak—and the rest of his life to learn to keep silent." That is a lesson needed for good interpersonal relationships on campus as well as at home. The Holy Spirit, our teacher, will in answer to our prayer set a guard upon our speech and help us to control it.

 Lord, keep a guard over my lips to protect others from my impulsive speech.

Make a practice of counting to 10 before you let your words and emotions fuse in audible speech.

■ KEEP IT SIMPLE

Eccles. 7:29: "God made us plain and simple, but we have made ourselves very complicated" (TEV).

To live a simple life, to be a simple person, demands a constant struggle. Our entire society—economic, social, political—is designed to add complexity to our daily existence. Busy students, trying to pack into a few flying years of education all the opportunities available to them, soon experience the hassle of complexity. Some who could do excellent work if they could hold to simplicity have frazzled nerves and delinquent work because they try to do everything in sight instead of choosing wisely among options. Those who see a virtue in simplicity need constantly to sluff off that which eats up time, energy, and resources.

Kipling's persona in one of his poems prays, "Teach us delight in simple things." What can have more value than the hug of a friend, the refreshment of a glass of cold water, the truth that "Jesus loves me, this I know"? A skill well worth developing is "Keep it simple." When God designed a way to draw human beings closer to himself God kept it simple—though not easy. The good news is a simple story of love and mercy.

 Lord, help me treasure the simple things of life.

Decide on at least two things you can do to uncomplicate your weekly schedule.

■ PROVING BY OUR LIVES

James 3:13-18: "Who is wise and understanding among you? Let him show it by his good life" (v. 13).

At a session at which students planned an evening at a nearby state park for which they would need drivers, they razzed their advisor mercilessly about his high-speed driving. Finally, one of the young men in the group put it to him bluntly. "John, how do you reconcile your being a Christian leader on campus with your reputation as a speed-demon driver?" John answered angrily, "There's no connection at all." But it was easy to see that his witness with that group had been badly impaired.

We need to forgive others and not condemn. But whenever a Christian engages in reckless or irresponsible behavior, the church bleeds a little and loses some of its credibility before the world.

James clearly associated wisdom and understanding with the living of a life pleasing to God. So should we. God's favor is ours not because we live a perfect life, but because of God's mercy and love. In response we let Christ work out in us a life that is a credit to his gospel.

 Lord, sensitize my conscience. Please keep my life from discrediting your kingdom in this world.

Take time to commit your daily habits and life to God in prayer.

■ PRINCE OF PEACE

Isa. 2:1-5:   "Let us walk in the light of the Lord"
(v. 5).

A cause about which young people the whole world over should be concerned is peace. No one has as much at stake in peace as do the young. They have always been the ones sent to fight the wars that older generations, greed, and the lust for power have brought about. If only the young of every nation could at the same moment say, "No, world, we will no longer be your cannon fodder!"

University campuses around the world have often been scenes of violence set off by a variety of causes, some idealistic and others chauvinistic or selfish. What a wonderful reversal it would be if instead the campuses of the world could throb with efforts to bring about peace, to curb the results of greed, to say a firm "no" to the lust for power.

Every one of us is called to that office of peacemaker in God's world. But until that end is achieved, Jesus promises us: "Peace I leave with you; my peace I give you. I do not give to you as the world gives. Do not let your hearts be troubled and do not be afraid" (John 14:27).

 Prince of Peace, show me how to become the peacemaker that you would have me be.

Make a deliberate effort to get to know and befriend a foreign student on your campus.

■ IF ONLY

Isa. 48:17-22: "If only you had paid attention to my commands, your peace would have been like a river, your righteousness like the waves of the sea" (v. 18).

How impressed were you in your childhood when your parents, trying to encourage you to do some desirable thing, said, "It's for your own good"? I don't remember being very convinced by that argument. Yet here God is saying the same thing.

If only! What common words these are, not only on college campuses, but in our world as a whole! "If only . . . I had studied harder for that test." "If only . . . I had listened to Dad when he told me I would need to budget my money." "If only . . . I hadn't let my date get too serious so fast." "If only . . . I had refused that last drink." "If only . . . I had been more responsible on the job." For every "If only" is implied the consequence with which the speaker now has to live, much to his or her regret. How much better things might have gone if one had weighed those consequences more carefully!

When God says "It's for your good" it is best to listen. After all, no one loves us with a love like his. We can trust that love to work for our good all the days of our lives.

 Lord, give me hearing ears, and help me to keep them open when you speak.

How can we be of help to others concerning matters mentioned above without coming across as preachy or moralistic?

■ OF WHAT DO YOU BOAST?

Jer. 9:23-24: "Let him who boasts boast about this:. that he understands and knows me" (v. 24).

Some individuals are very aggressive, having a need to be recognized by all around them. At the other extreme are those who are content to stay in the background, seemingly unconcerned about recognition.

One can certainly understand a boaster's motivation. We all need some of the ego-reinforcement that recognition of our achievements gives us. We all need enough self-confidence to be able to say, "I'm good at this," or "This is one of my strong points." We also need enough modesty so that we do not constantly bombard others with our own wonderfulness. Modesty about one's abilities is easier for us to admire in others than to practice for ourselves. Finding the right mix of self-confidence and humility is important in college as we begin to look ahead to working with employers and colleagues.

If we need something about which to boast, we always have at hand God's goodness and love, dependability and righteousness.

 Lord, give me the right blend of confidence and humility.

Try looking at yourself today as if you were in someone else's shoes.

■ THE POTTER AND THE CLAY

Jer. 18:1-7: "Like clay in the hand of the potter, so are you in my hand" (v. 6).

Have you ever wandered around the classrooms of the art department, looking at the sculpture, the watercolors, or the ceramics in process? Perhaps, like me, you are hard put to explain what you are seeing. We need not worry about that. Sometimes the seeing is enough in itself.

One of the studios I like to look into is the ceramics one. Splat! goes a blob of clay on the wheel, and the long careful process begins until that earthen mud becomes a graceful vase with a handle and a lip and a glaze.

Both Isaiah and Jeremiah used the image of the potter and the clay to be a model of God's shaping of the people of Israel. If you have prayed that your life be fashioned for God's purposes, you can have faith that when you do an experiment in a laboratory, read in a library carrel, train in a gymnasium, God is molding you, taking a rough edge off here, refining a talent there. You may not realize until years later the usefulness of some of those times when the master potter put your half-formed clay back on the wheel and began to fashion you again for his glory.

 Great Potter, fashion my life to suit what is your will for me.

As you think about your own life, take time today to watch a person throw a pot and shape or correct it.

■ VERBALLY COMMITTED

1 John 2:14-19: "I write to you, young men, because you are strong, and the word of God lives in you, and you have overcome the evil one" (v. 14).

Many of us are fearful of being thought dogmatic, possessed of ideas set in cement. Often it seems preferable to be reluctant or unable to express a strong conviction or to have a determined loyalty. A few are so afraid of conflicting opinions being expressed in a conversation that real exchange of ideas from which one can learn or be stimulated to think becomes impossible, and nothing worthwhile is ever sorted out in their presence.

John would not have been very much at ease with such people, nor would Peter, Paul, or James. John saw life as a continuous making of choices between what belongs to "the world" and what comes from the Father. He did not portray believers as Milquetoasts, forever afraid their decisions might be minority ones. Living John's way calls us to be people who have the courage of our beliefs and the knowledge to defend them. The young people to whom John wrote had, through the Word and the Spirit that lived in them and also lives in us, learned to be strong in their convictions.

 Lord, give me the courage of my convictions and the grace to defend them with tact and love, but also with firmness.

Make a list of five of your personal convictions about which you are confident enough to be willing to speak before others.

■ IN GOD I HOPE

Lam. 3:21-23: "Yet this I call to mind and therefore I have hope: Because of the Lord's great love we are not consumed, for his compassions never fail. They are new every morning" (vv. 2l-23).

Some scientists predict that a nuclear winter would follow any nuclear war. Talk shows discuss the catastrophe that will occur if we do not begin to conserve our water resources. A newspaper headline screams, "Death Star may cause extinction of life."

Many of today's doomsayers are researchers from the academic community, busy setting up their own hypotheses and knocking over those of others. One of the dangers of such doomsaying is that we may become numb to these prophecies and not do what we can to avert their coming true. Remember the boy who cried wolf so often that no one listened when the wolf really appeared?

Despair comes all too easily to us human beings. Yet, with the writer of Lamentations, we can have hope in the Lord's "great love . . . and compassions." The hope God gives us for the future frees us to do the work that is necessary to prevent catastrophes from taking place.

 Lord, I am grateful that among all the doomsayers I can still believe in your love and mercy.

Choose a cause related to the problems that face us in the future. Get involved now and help do something about it.

■ TESTING THE SPIRITS

1 John 4:1-6: "Many false prophets have gone out into the world" (v. 1).

If you haven't done it yourself you have no doubt watched a science student examining a substance in a test tube, seeking to separate its elements. One can sense among the New Testament writers a concern that new believers learn to separate truth from falsehood, to recognize the false prophets of the day and reject their teachings.

Just as litmus paper identifies the presence of acid, so the giving of the proper position to Jesus Christ, John says, is the touchstone of the true prophet. That rules out those who tell us that Jesus was one of many prophets to be equally honored, who say he was an admirable teacher of high moral standards, but nothing more than that.

Old Testament believers had several criteria by which they separated the false prophets from the true. St. John named only one test: Jesus is attested as the Christ by the witness of God's Spirit to his coming in the flesh to do the Father's will. And that Spirit tells the truth.

O God, among all the voices I hear, help me to recognize only those who tell the truth about you.

Watch the bulletin boards on your campus to see what "prophets" are calling for your attention. Which do not meet the criterion set up by John?

■ A PERSONAL CHALLENGE

Jude 14-25:   "Keep yourself in God's love (v. 21).

One of the cardinal rules for studying the Bible is to compare Scripture with Scripture, to compare what is said in one part with what is said elsewhere. When we do that, we need to keep what we have read in context or we may have seeming contradictions on our hands. Two authors may be engaged in developing different ideas when what they say seems opposite in meaning.

For example, Jude told his readers to "Keep yourselves in God's love," while Paul reassured *his* readers that "he who began a good work" in them would "carry it on to completion until the day of Christ Jesus" (Phil. 1:6). God's love is a gift God bestows by grace, a gift that is not a result of our own efforts. Jude's verse is puzzling.

Is one of these statements right and the other wrong? Not at all. Each is part of a longer statement, the verse from Jude prefaced by, "Pray in the Holy Spirit." *There* is the power for keeping yourself in the love of God. The command in Phil. 2:12 is followed by the reminder that God is working *in* the believer who is then to work *out* what God has worked *in*.

 Lord, make me cooperative with what you are doing in my life.

Go back to verse 3 in Jude. How can you relate that to what is said above?

■ A BETTER IDEA

Eph. 5:8-20: "Do not get drunk on wine . . . .
Instead, be filled with the Spirit" (v. 18).

It is still fairly common to see intoxication portrayed
as comical. The figure of the jovial, staggering drunk is
almost guaranteed to get a laugh out of an audience.

The reality of chemical dependency, however, is not
nearly so funny. Alcoholism is a progressive disease
that is both addictive and destructive. And it is a
serious problem for some college students. We still
know far too little about the causes and treatment of
alcoholism. Yet we do know how important it is for
friends, relatives, and employers to face the facts of
addiction and not make excuses for an alcoholic. Often
it is only by working together that they can intervene
and get a victim of this disease to seek treatment.

Paul offered an alternative to the destructive
"partying" that is so common on college campuses.
The Spirit of God can fill our human spirits,
eliminating the need to drown our pain and boredom
in chemical "highs." The Spirit is God's free gift to
Christians, and living in the Spirit never produces
illness or a hangover!

 God, give me the joy of living that your Spirit
can bring.

**Do you know someone who shows signs of chemical
dependency? Is there a way you can help him or her
obtain treatment?**

■ THE POUTER

Jonah 4: "He made himself a shelter, sat in its shade and waited to see what would happen to the city" (v. 5).

When wicked Nineveh had become repentant Nineveh—with even the cattle forced to fast and wear sackcloth—Jonah sat pouting. Jonah, who knew of God's mercy, resented that mercy when it was extended to others.

Jonah went on pouting, even after he was reproved by God. There is no evidence that this pouting prophet ever repented of his childish, petty grumpiness about God being merciful to people Jonah disliked.

It is not only children who find it hard to stop pouting. So do many adults. They pout over poor grades, even when they were deserved; they pout over being left out, over being given too much—or too little—responsibility. God directs the same question at us as at Jonah: "What right do you have to be angry?" All too often our answers make no more sense than Jonah's. Christian maturity includes putting pouting aside. How much better to find the truth in what God says, thank him, and by God's guidance accept his ways.

 God, help me to be mature enough so that I do not sulk.

Try to identify the kinds of situations that most tempt you to sulk, and then keep alert to the danger.

■ BUT SUPPOSE HE *MEANT* THEM?

Matt. 5:38-48: "Love your enemies and pray for those who persecute you" (v. 44).

Some teachings of Jesus call for attitudes so different from usual human views that our reaction to them has been, "Oh, but of course he didn't really *mean* that!" Think of Matthew 5, with its paradoxical statements in the Beatitudes, its equation of hatred with murder, and its command that we love our enemies. People often react to these verses by spiritualizing them, moving them into a rarified abstract context so that they need not be taken seriously.

Isn't it rather strange to insist that the one who prayed "Father, forgive them for they do not know what they are doing" (Luke 23:34) did not really mean it when he commanded us not to seek revenge on those who wrong us?

Just suppose Jesus *did* mean exactly what he said and expects us to take him seriously? Where does that leave us who inhabit campuses which claim to be involved in the search for truth? What *did* Jesus mean when in effect he said we are to have no enemies? For if we love them, they are no longer enemies. Do you suppose he meant us to take him straight?

 Lord, help me not to try to reason your words away.

Read Rom. 12:17-21. Note that Jesus is not the only one in the Bible who asks us to accept difficult challenges.

■ IN PRAISE OF WISDOM

Prov. 8:22-31:   "The Lord possessed me at the beginning of his work, before his deeds of old" (v. 22).

A long poem in praise of wisdom dominates the first nine chapters of Proverbs. Wisdom, personified as a woman, says she was the Creator's constant companion in the establishment and ordering of the earth.

Wisdom is more than facts: it couples knowledge with understanding and integrity. It does not grow out of our narrow specializations; it distills out of the breadth of our searching of many fields of study. It is refined out of God's word shaping our attitudes as we seek to develop a well-rounded view of the world and the human beings who live on it and call it home.

The development of such wisdom is part of the reason for that part of our college education we call the liberal arts. Our education leads us into a vocation or a profession, but it also leads us to understand and cherish the good earth God has given us and to live harmoniously with others on it. Wisdom is God's gift to his children, apportioned to us in and outside of academic education. To achieve it we need to submit our human minds to the light God's Spirit turns on for us.

 Lord, grace my education, please, with the gift of your wisdom.

Have you read C. S. Lewis's *Pilgrim's Regress?* If not, read it as a way of sharing in one individual's search for wisdom.

■ READY FOR THE EXODUS

Isa. 43:1-5: "When you pass through the waters, I will be with you" (v. 2).

There is something in almost all of us that tends to draw back from new ventures, that wants both to reach forward to the new and to cling for support to the tried and the familiar.

We shed tears at our high school graduation, even while we eagerly anticipate college. We hesitate to commit ourselves to a challenge at the same time we hope our audition was good enough to get us into the concert choir, or our performance stellar enough to make the team. It's sort of a relief that someone else has the last word in the decision. When we come to the end of campus life, something in us would like to be that "professional student" who keeps hanging around the university. But at the same time we know it is time to move out into the world of our career.

How comforting that the same promises that upheld the Hebrews now come from God to us! God nudges us out, away from the comfortably familiar. God promises to be with us.

 Lord, loosen my fingers from what I should leave behind and give me guidance in what lies ahead.

What in your past do you find most appealing to hold on to at the same time as you know you need to let it go to move forward?

BIBLE READINGS SERIES

Bible Readings for Women
Lyn Klug

Bible Readings for Men
Steve Swanson

Bible Readings for Couples
Margaret and Erling Wold

Bible Readings for Singles
Ruth Stenerson

Bible Readings for Families
Mildred and Luverne Tengbom

Bible Readings for Parents
Ron and Lyn Klug

Bible Readings for Teenagers
Charles S. Mueller

Bible Readings for Teachers
Ruth Stenerson

Bible Readings for Church Workers
Harry N. Huxhold

Bible Readings for the Retired
Leslie F. Brandt

Bible Readings for Troubled Times
Leslie F. Brandt

Bible Readings for Growing Christians
Kevin E. Ruffcorn

Bible Readings for Farm Living
Frederick Baltz

Bible Readings on Prayer
Ron Klug